THE WONDERFUL WORLD OF DOGS

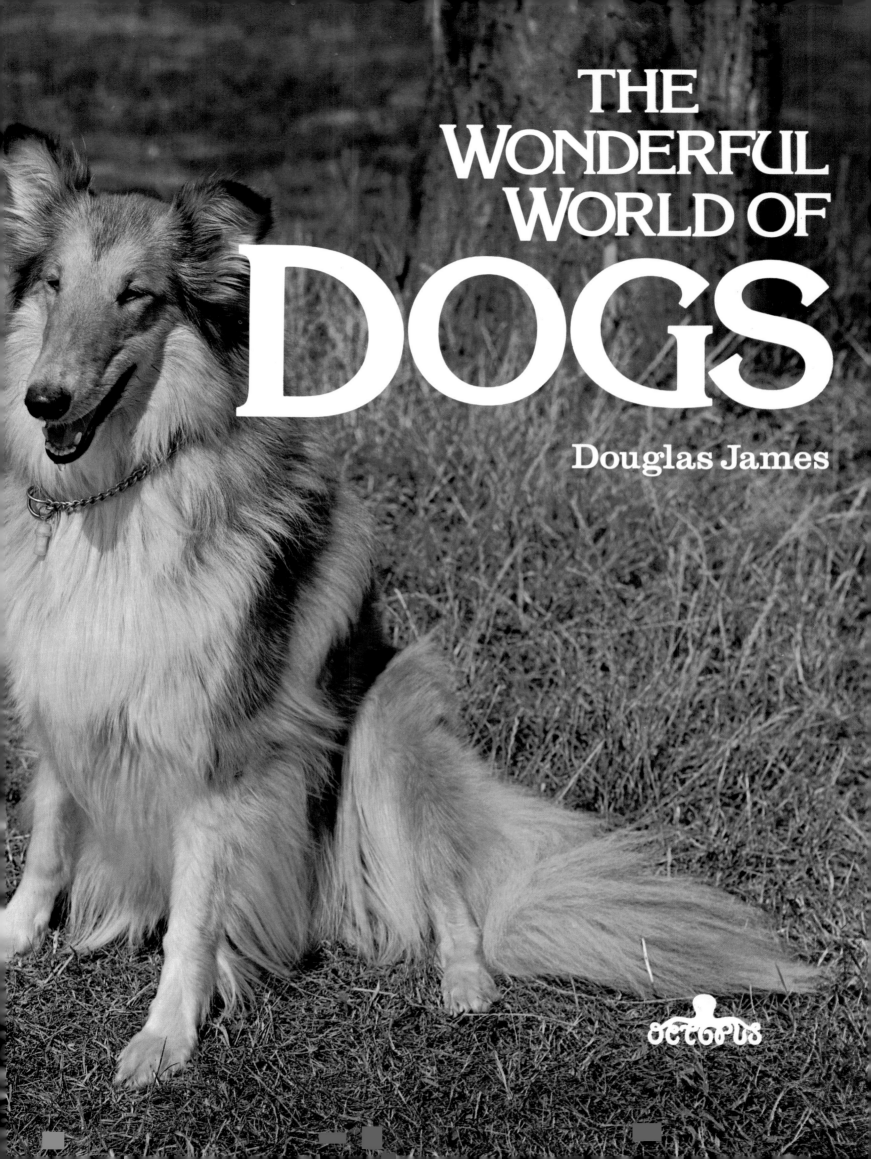

THE WONDERFUL WORLD OF DOGS

Douglas James

OCTOPUS

CONTENTS

First published 1976 by
Octopus Books Limited
59 Grosvenor Street, London W1

ISBN 0 7064 0562 5

© 1976 Octopus Books Limited

Produced by Mandarin Publishers Limited
22a Westlands Road, Quarry Bay, Hong Kong

Printed in Hong Kong

CHOOSING A DOG

There is no animal that has a relationship with man as close as that of the dog. This companionship has always been appreciated, although all of us might not want to go as far as the first-century Greek historian Arrian, who said 'Nothing is so helpful for the dog as a warm, soft bed. It is best of all if they can sleep with a person, because it makes them more human, and because they rejoice in the company of human beings.'

Rejoicing in the company of humans is perhaps the dog's greatest asset. When the family was a large unit, everyone had a chance of finding someone with the time to give them affection, offer them sympathy and listen to their troubles. With smaller families and less leisure, loneliness is an ever-present, ever-growing problem and the uncritical flattery of the pet dog often affords some sort of consolation for a largely indifferent world. Talking to the dog may be a poor substitute for talking to another human being, but it is certainly better than talking to oneself. This companionship is often under-estimated, for the loyal adulation of the family pet can be of great value to the child who is feeling unjustly misunderstood or who is consumed with jealousy.

Pet dogs fulfil many functions for their owners and have the advantage that they can be ignored when they are not needed. You do not have to be on your best behaviour with the dog. You can take out your anger and frustration on it and it will be glad to see you just the same. Many people like the dependency of keeping a dog. The urge to feed and care for someone or something is a very fundamental one and a dog will never become independent or be ungrateful. To pet and fondle an animal can be a sensual tactile pleasure and the dog will make no demands in return. The pet dog fulfils different needs for different owners and with the stresses of modern life these needs seem to grow more rather than less.

Unfortunately all owners do not consider the dog's needs as well as their own. Primarily the dog is a social animal which should not be left alone every day when the family goes out to work. A bored and lonely dog can be both noisy and destructive, so if you have to be out all the time it is better to choose some other pet which is less demanding in this respect. A dog needs a diet suited to its own needs, and this means a fairly high proportion of that expensive commodity, meat. A surprising number of owners buy a dog they cannot afford to feed. A dog also needs daily exercise and this depends on the owner's time and energy. No dog should be allowed to roam. The town stray fouls the pavements and causes traffic accidents. The country dog on the loose also causes accidents and there is always the danger that it will end up chasing someone else's stock on someone else's land and get shot. If it seems impossible to keep your dog at home, except when it is being exercised by someone, then, again, choose some less demanding pet. The dog needs to be kept clean and well groomed and someone has got to be responsible for this. If you are attracted by the glamour of a long-coated breed, remember that ten minutes of regular daily attention is going to be needed to preserve that eye-catching appearance. Finally the dog is going to need a certain amount of training, both for your sake and the sake of the community.

You may want to keep a dog for any number of reasons but the people around you may not be animal lovers. They may be indifferent or hostile but their rights should be respected. Your dog should not be allowed to foul the pavements or footpaths. It should not be allowed to bark continually nor to frighten people by boisterous or aggressive behaviour. A well-trained dog will never be a nuisance in ways like these.

Your choice of dog should be dictated by the amount of space you have, the amount of time you are willing to spend and the amount of money you can spare to meet the weekly food bill. But even within this framework there is an enormous variety of breeds and types from which to choose.

The variety of shape, size, colouring and marking shown in the hundreds of different breeds of dog that there are in the world make it difficult to believe that there is a common ancestor behind them all. It is fascinating to speculate where all these differences came from and how each one became established as a characteristic peculiar to a certain breed. Why do Chows have black tongues? Why is it, when most puppies are born fully marked at birth, the spots on the Dalmatian only start to appear when the litter is two or three weeks old? Why, when many dogs have no dew-claws on their hind legs, do Pyrenean Mountain dogs (Great Pyrenées) have two? Breeds like these have been established so long that no one knows when these distinctive features occurred or how they became established.

Originally nearly all dogs were useful and bred specifically for the work they had to do. Because travelling was difficult and communications poor or non-existent, the sheepdogs in one part of the country could differ markedly in looks from animals doing the same job a couple of hundred miles away. Though looks and working ability are not necessarily closely con-

The Shetland Sheepdog *(right)*, originally a working dog, is now established as a very popular pet. It is not a specially created miniature, although only 14 in. high, but like the Shetland Pony and the sheep and cattle of the Shetland Islands is a natural adaptation to their environment.

The Schnauzer type was established as a watchdog in Germany early in the seventeenth century but although used for police work in its native land, it is hardly known elsewhere. The standard size is a general purpose

The Cavalier King Charles Spaniel (*above*) is one of the most popular toy dogs in Great Britain, possibly because it combines a small compact size with a distinctly sporting character. This breed was re-created in the 1920s due to the enthusiasm of an American. He offered British breeders a prize if they could produce the type of toy spaniel seen in contemporary portraits of Charles II. This led to the rebirth of the Cavalier, a breed which ironically is scarcely known in the States. Princess Margaret's patronage of the breed has further increased its popularity.

nected, it is a natural assumption to link the two together. Thus all the vermin killing terriers of one Yorkshire dale would be black and tan while, further to the south, white dogs patched with black or brown would be doing the same job. Beyond stating that these early regional differences provided the basis for different breeds, we can say little more with certainty until we come to the nineteenth century when various new breeds were deliberately created and we know a little more about the methods used.

With so many types to choose from you can suit your personal taste in the matter of your pet's looks and, to a certain extent, in the matter of its temperament. This is one of the main advantages the pure-bred animal has over the mongrel. If you choose a pedigree puppy, you will know the size to which it will grow and how it will look when adult. You will even have some idea of the type of temperament to expect. With a mongrel all this is much more of a gamble. The initial cost of a pure-bred animal will be more, but this difference in cost spread over the ten years or so of a dog's life is little enough to pay for a certain pride in ownership. With a pedigree dog you may even be tempted into the show ring and discover a new and fascinating world. You may also find that training your dog gives you so much satisfaction that you will want to enter obedience competitions. Either of these activities will increase your pride and pleasure and deepen the bond between dog and owner. Whatever your personal preference in looks and character, you should be able to find it somewhere among the hundred or so different breeds available. From then on what you make of the companionship of your dog is up to you.

working dog and the Miniature Schnauzer *(left)* is a very popular pet on both sides of the Atlantic with its harsh, wiry coat and prominent moustache and whiskers. Although terrier-like in appearance (and classified as a terrier in the United States) it has none of the terrier's aggressiveness and excitability.

The Sealyham Terrier *(right)* was created over a hundred years ago in southern Wales to be a fearless fellow capable of tackling any kind of vermin. It gets its name from the country estate where it was developed by an eccentric sportsman who bred his own terriers for dealing with otters and polecats. Since then the Sealyham has been smartened up in appearance and its somewhat foolhardy temperament has been toned down to more reasonable proportions. This breed often prove very comical characters and their devotees claim that Sealyhams have a good sense of humour. They are tremendously popular in the United States but in Britain can scarcely muster a tenth of the numbers of the West Highland White. It remains a mystery why one short-legged white terrier should be so much more popular than another.

The raggle-taggle charm of the Bearded Collie *(below)* has only recently been appreciated. The breed, used for working both sheep and cattle in the Scottish hills, was not recognized as pure-bred until 1948, when the first one was registered with the Kennel Club. They are active dogs, racily built under a weather-resistant shaggy coat which insulates them from cold and wet. Their love of life, their curiosity and their desire to please make them excellent family pets for those who want an intelligent and energetic dog.

Its rich mahogany red colour and attractive long coat make the Irish Setter *(left)* a distinctive breed. Although only the red colouring is now recognized this setter was once both red and white and dogs of the old type are still found in Ireland.

Dogs like this, bred to go out with the sportsman, quarter the ground for game and stand steady when they have scented it, need exercise and work to do. Because their coat is flat and glossy they do not require too much grooming.

Cats and dogs are not always antagonistic as many households with both kinds of pet can testify. A dog who grows up with a cat—especially if they are young together, or if an older dog has a young kitten companion —will treat it as one of his pack, even if he thinks every other feline in the neighbourhood is an enemy!
The Pyrenean Mountain Dog puppies *(above right)* look small furry bundles but many people falling in love with them at the breeder's kennels forget that they do not stay like that for long. When they are fully grown they may weigh as much as 100 to 125 lb and stand anything from 25 to 32 in. at the shoulder. These majestic and noble dogs originated in France where they were used to guard the shepherd and his sheep. All-white in colour, some with a few markings of badger-grey or carrying shades of tan, they have a dense undercoat with a long thick outer coat and need good grooming to keep it in order. Large dogs like these must not be over-indulged and should be taught from the start of your ownership. They are extremely intelligent and quick to learn.

Beagles are one of the oldest British breeds. They are as gay and lively when adult as when they are puppies *(right)*. They love to hunt and enjoy access to fields where they can gallop as they should. Like most 'pack' breeds, they can be deaf to all commands when they choose. It is therefore important to teach them strict obedience when they are small. They are short-coated and so do not trail mud into the house, and need a minimum of grooming. Even when fully grown they are not very big, growing to 16 in. at the highest.

In some breeds the adult dog may bear little resemblance to the puppy. Changes of coat colour as a dog grows older are often dramatic and not always entirely predictable. This dark brown and white Bearded Collie puppy *(left)* may end up as light a shade as its mother when its adult coat finally comes through. All Old English Sheepdogs are born black and white and only become grey or grizzled later in life. Liver Bedlington Terriers are born dark brown and change to a light biscuit shade. Even the spots on the Dalmatian are not there at birth, only beginning to appear as dark smudges at about three weeks.

The Pekingese *(below)* is one of the most popular toy dogs in the world. The romantic story of how four of these dogs were found by British troops during the looting of the Imperial Palace in Peking in 1860 caught the public's fancy. One of these, 'Looty', was presented to Queen Victoria. This, however, would not have been enough to establish the breed so firmly. It was the character of a dog which combined dignity with exasperating stubbornness, and comical charm with playfulness, that ensured its popularity with so many people. All the Pekingese in the West are descended from those first four dogs and a few more smuggled out of China at the turn of the century. They are tough and sturdy animals with profuse coats which can be any shade.

The little Papillon *(above)* is a member of the dwarf spaniel family. The large fringed ears, carried obliquely, suggest the wings of a butterfly, as the French name implies, and a well-defined white blaze on the face represents the body of the insect. A rarer type with drop ears shows more clearly the relationship to toy spaniels. These dogs were favourites at the French court where their small size and high spirits were much valued. They have a flowing coat but it is easy to manage as it has no undercoat.

The aristocratic Deerhound *(right)* is a dog whose history is so closely interwoven with that of Scotland that it might almost be called the national breed. A powerful and dignified animal, the appearance of the Deerhound has altered little over the last 150 years, although their numbers have fluctuated alarmingly during that period. Ownership was once restricted to persons of the rank of Earl or higher and it was the companion of Highland Chieftains, but its numbers dwindled when the clan system collapsed. The enthusiasm of Queen Victoria and eminent Victorians such as the painter Landseer revived its popularity. Originally the hounds were bred for strength and stamina to overtake wounded stags and bring them to bay. With the development of the sporting rifle, the need for such hounds grew less and their numbers subsequently declined.

The Borzoi *(below)*, like the Deerhound, was bred for speed. They should be at least 29 in. tall and move with a light, free action. The long silky coat can be any colour. Their alternative name—Russian Wolfhound—gives a clue to the breed's origins. One of the favourite sports of the Imperial Court of the Russian Empire was coursing the wolf. The Czars and the Russian nobility kept enormous numbers of hounds with which to indulge their taste for a rather formalized type of hunting where hounds were loosed in pairs to bring wolves to bay. The Russian Revolution would have ended the breed as such had it not already been established in Britain and the United States by the end of the nineteenth century.

The Saluki *(above right)*, pure-bred by the Arabs for many generations, was introduced into Britain in the last century. Somewhat smaller than the Borzoi and with perhaps an even more elegant silky coat it can run extremely fast. Naturally they need space in which to exercise. A graceful and attractive dog looking very like the Saluki has been portrayed on Assyrian and Babylonian bas-reliefs, on Classical Greek vases and in Renaissance oil paintings and tapestries. They have been known round the Mediterranean throughout history and were the favourite hounds of the nomadic desert sheiks who used them for hunting gazelle, often in partnership with falcons. So favoured a dog were they that they are said to be the only ones the Arabs would allow in their tents, the rest of the canine race being considered unclean. They have a charming and very faithful character and make very desirable household companions— but like other regal and dignified breeds should not be made fun of!

The Doberman Pinscher *(right)* has gained great popularity in recent years. It is shining black with tan, brown or blue markings and stands 25 to 27 in. high. They require plenty of exercise and lots of human attention. The breed is used as a police and Army dog, particularly in the United States, and has the reputation of having a very suspicious nature and very quick reactions. This breed was the creation of one man, Louis Dobermann, who wanted a guard dog *par excellence*. In the 1870s, in Germany, he crossed a number of local breeds to get the type he wanted. Since then some of the ferocity which made the breed noted in its early years has been bred out and the Doberman is now a stable, intelligent dog as well as a first-class guard dog.

The tiny Chihuahua *(left)* should not exceed a weight of 6 lb. The breed originated in Mexico and comes in both smooth-coated and long-coated varieties.

In contrast the Great Dane *(below)* is remarkable for its size. It is an ideal companion and guard for those who can afford to feed it and although muscular and very strong is usually docile when properly treated. Despite its name this dog is a native of Germany where it was used to hunt wild boar.

The Hungarian Vizsla *(right)* is a solid-coloured gun dog which ranges through shades from rusty gold to dark sandy yellow. It is a powerfully built dog with a partially docked tail and a lithe, well-balanced gait.

The Basenji *(below right)* is one of the oldest hunting dogs and was well known to the Pharaohs of ancient Egypt. This is a lightly built dog with a gazelle-like grace, distinctive pricked ears, a tightly curled tail and wrinkled forehead. Recently rediscovered by Europeans in the Congo, Basenjis were used there to hunt all the smaller types of equatorial game. Running mute, the dogs had wooden bells hung round their necks so that their native owners could track them when they were hidden by the tall elephant grass. They are unusual in that they do not bark, making chortling and yodelling noises instead.

17

PUPPIES

Puppies are born relatively undeveloped and helpless and need a high degree of maternal care to survive. A bitch will want to give birth in a safe, secluded den. Many have dug a burrow and farm dogs, for example, will tunnel into haystacks to make a warm, insulated den. The best kind of whelping box, therefore, is one which is low enough for the mother just to be able to stand and the door of the box just big enough for her to get through. This enclosed space will satisfy the bitch's need for safety, seclusion and darkness. The floor space should be large enough for her to stretch out flat on her side. The top should be removable so that the puppies can be looked at and reached if anything goes wrong.

All puppies, whatever their breed, look much the same at birth. They are blind and deaf and covered with short sleek fur. Their muzzles are blunt, and their ears folded and crumpled. Their legs seem too small for their bodies and cannot yet support the puppy's weight. Birth weight differences between breeds are not so great as the differences in size of the adult dogs might lead one to expect. A puppy of a toy breed might weigh 4 oz at birth and grow up to be a 6 lb adult, thus increasing its body weight 24 times. A puppy of a much larger breed might well weigh 2 lb when born and weigh 100 lb when adult, an increase of 50 times. This is one of the reasons why large breeds are slower to develop and mature. The small dog may be fully grown by eight months but one of the giant breeds will not be mature until two and a half or three years of age. Because big dogs need extra food for growth over such a long time, they are even more expensive to keep than many people realize.

Two things are vital for very young puppies: food and warmth. All animals have methods to keep their body temperature constant even though the temperature of their surroundings may alter, but for the first few days of their lives puppies have not yet developed this ability. At this stage they are more like reptiles and their body temperature varies according to the temperature of their surroundings. Only constant contact with its mother keeps a puppy warm. She will remain with her newborn litter and cannot normally be persuaded to leave them for more than a minute or two.

Puppies who cannot find their mother to snuggle close to begin to cry and crawl round in circles. If their distress calls do not bring the mother back, their movements and their body functions get slower as they get colder and colder. The heart does not beat as fast and they cannot digest any food they may be given. Paradoxically this cataleptic state may be an asset to survival in the wild where puppies which were noisy and active during their mother's absence might endanger themselves by attracting the attention of predators.

Puppies are born with the so-called 'rooting reflex'. This causes the puppy to push towards a teat almost as soon as it is born. It will burrow under other members of the litter with surprising strength and persistence. The tongue of a young puppy is curved like a scoop, making a very efficient sucking mechanism. While the puppies are feeding, they also knead the mother's milk glands with their front paws to stimulate the supply.

Most puppies open their eyes between the tenth and fourteenth day of life. Like kittens and most human babies their eyes are blue and do not function very well at first. By the eighth or ninth week they will have darkened to the adult colour. During the third week the puppies begin to hear and to show interest in their litter mates and in people. They learn to wag their tails and their legs are now strong enough to support their body weight. The puppies begin to bark and growl and to attempt to play with each other and with their mother. The instinct to keep the nest clean is inborn and as soon as the puppy can walk it will move away from the sleeping area before relieving itself. This instinct is the one we want to foster when we housetrain a puppy.

Mock fighting begins at this stage among the litter and establishes which puppy will be leader. Normally this is the biggest male as in the wild, but in a litter of bitch puppies it is often the noisiest female. The mother disciplines the litter, growling and nipping if they pester her unduly or are too rough in their play. There is evidence to suggest that if a puppy misses this period of play with its litter mates and its mother, it may never have a normal relationship with other dogs when it is adult. It may become a life-long bully or a coward. Between the third and fifth week of a puppy's life it must have human contact for the man/dog relationship to become fixed. Once the bond has been established by contact at this critical period in the puppy's life, it can never be entirely broken.

These lively young Golden Retriever puppies *(right)* have the gun dog's instincts in their blood and will enjoy being taught to retrieve even if they are kept only as household pets.

Like all young animals, puppies need plenty of uninterrupted rest—like this West Highland White *(above)*—if they are to grow and flourish. Healthy puppies are either eating, playing or utterly relaxed in the appealing sleep of babyhood. This exhausted yellow Labrador mother *(above right)* snoozes beside her puppies, although at this stage the bitch often likes to get a little peace by sleeping away from the litter. A floor covering of newspaper is the most economical for puppies reared indoors, as it can be changed at frequent intervals.

When they are four weeks old puppies will probably try to climb out of their box and begin to explore the world and weaning should already have begun. Give them an enclosed space to play in to make sure they do not stray too far but ensure that they get plenty of light and air. They will want to play but do not let them get over-exhausted. Young puppies need plenty of sleep. These Foxhound pups *(right)* in kennels still seem a little wary of the world.

These Standard Poodle puppies *(left)* with their mothers already have the characteristic curly coat. Even a couple of puppies can be a handful as any owner knows but many breeds frequently produce eight or more. A litter of eight is as much as any bitch should be asked to rear. In a number of continental countries where specialist clubs control the breeding of pedigree animals very strictly, six puppies is considered to be the maximum that should be left in a litter. Not only should the mother have unlimited good food, the puppies themselves may need supplementary feeding as well as extra-early weaning.

From the moment of birth, puppies are the most ruthless egoists. These week-old Golden Retriever puppies *(below left)* are still deaf and blind, for their eyes and ears will not function until they are 10 to 12 days old. All puppies, however, are born with the rooting reflex which ensures that they nuzzle towards a teat for the all-important life-giving milk within minutes of birth. The favoured position is under the mother's hind leg where there is warmth and where the milk supply is more abundant. The strongest puppies will always be found in this position.

It seems no time at all before the newborn puppies have grown into mischievous imps like this confident little Jack Russell Terrier *(right)*.

Pointers *(left)* are a very fertile breed which often have large litters, but it is the largest breeds which tend to have the most puppies. It would not be unusual for a St Bernard *(below)* to have ten or more puppies in her litter. Feeding so many puppies is a very expensive business and their diet has to be more than adequate to maintain the necessary growth rate. Dogs like these have massive bones, and calcium and vitamin supplements are even more essential than usual. The average adult male St Bernard will weigh about 180 lb, and the highest recorded weight for one of the breed is 259 lb.

An Italian Greyhound suckles her pup *(above right)*.

Playing in the snow is fun for both this Samoyed puppy and his mother *(below right)*.

All growing puppies will benefit from sunshine and fresh air and will enjoy a day in the open like these yellow Labradors *(left)*.

Cocker Spaniels *(below)* are the most popular of all the spaniels but their coats require a lot of attention and they need careful disciplining when puppies to stop them from becoming jealous and over-possessive.

A German Shepherd Dog puppy *(right)* does not suggest the powerful dog it will be when fully grown. These are dogs that need firm control. They make excellent guard dogs and devoted companions but such powerful animals must be carefully trained in obedience. Teaching a puppy to be a tolerant and harmonious member of the household can hardly start too young.

SHEEP AND HERDING DOGS

Since man and dog first combined together as hunters, the partnership has more often than not been a working one, with man finding more and more uses for the dog as time went on. Man's superior brain has devised increasingly sophisticated applications of the dog's superior sense of hearing and smell, and the dog's superior speed, strength and stamina.

From hunting herds of grazing animals, man progressed to keeping his own domesticated flocks. One of the first domesticated animals was the reindeer and guarding and herding them was the adaptable dog. Sheepdogs can be divided into two types. There were the guard dogs, which were expected to keep off predators such as wolves. These dogs were left with the flocks, especially at night, and acted on their own initiative when danger threatened. The wild dog will defend its own territory; the domesticated dog, accepting man as the pack leader, will guard its master's belongings. Dogs like these could be left to keep the flocks in a designated area and when the sheep were moved from pasture to pasture the guard dogs led the way, rather than driving the flock from behind, the type of work done by the second type of sheepdog. The herding instinct, so strong in some working collies as to be almost a mania, is an adaptation of the hunting drives of the wild dog. Wolves driving herds of caribou will single out a weak member of the herd and kill it. The modern Border Collie working sheep shows all the movements of a hunting animal. The belly-to-the-ground crawl forward, the sudden short rush, the streaking run after a sheep that has broken away, all these are the movements of a predator stalking its prey. The fixed glare, which helps the sheepdog control the sheep and is known as showing 'eye', is paralleled by the keen, hypnotic stare of the hunting dog viewing the victim. As far as the sheepdog is concerned, it is only the final kill that is absent.

The pastoral dog is a member of a very ancient race. Sheepdogs were first used in Britain by the Brythonic Celts who owned great herds of cattle and thousands of sheep, although we do not know what kind of dog they used. Every country has bred a type suitable for local use, but one of the best known is the Scotch Collie which is the one most used in Britain and the United States, where the first specimens were introduced by the colonists, and has been exported to many parts of the world. The sheepdogs throughout the centuries were developed as the result of cross breeding between the Celtic dogs, the dogs brought into Britain by the Romans and, later, Anglo Saxon and Norman herding dogs, but the credit for the collie must be given to Scotland. It was known as early as the end of the

sixteenth century and illustrations dating *circa* 1790 show a collie very much like the modern sheepdog. The breed spread down through England and Wales, mainly as a result of the southern sheep farmers meeting the drovers who travelled most of the roads and tracks between England and Scotland. The working collie must not be confused with the Rough or Smooth Collies which are now popular as pets or on the show benches. These were certainly bred from the working dogs originally but are rarely, if ever, seen to work sheep.

One of the supreme sheepdogs of the world is the dog popularly known as the Border Collie. There is no standard of points for this clever dog since there is considerable variation of size and type. Intelligence and ability to work with sheep are the most important requirements, and since the owner of a bitch naturally chooses the best dog available, collies over the generations have become one of the purest breeds in the British Isles. There are smooth and rough coated types, some are slightly built to enable them to cover hill country, while a heavier variety would be able to work on flat pastures without exhaustion—and a sheepdog must work all day from dawn to dusk.

A sheepdog starts training from six months of age onwards. It is not true that a puppy is trained by allowing it to run with an experienced collie, and individual training by the shepherd is necessary—left to the older dog the pup would be more likely to pick up bad habits than useful instruction!

The sheepdogs of Hungary are hairy specimens of ancient origin specially bred to work long hours on the windswept plains of Hungary. The chief breeds are the Komondor, Puli and Kuvask, and specimens of each can be seen in Britain and the United States. The supreme sheepdog of Italy is the Maremma, a white dog of some 25 in. at the shoulder and resembling the Komondor, with which it shares a common ancestry.

The Briard of France is a big shaggy dog, while the Bouvier des Flandres stands 28 in. at the shoulder and is a cattle driving dog. The Germans think highly of the German Shepherd Dog, also known as the Alsatian in Britain, which is one of the oldest herding breeds in the world, and has the double job of working sheep with the shepherd and keeping the flock off the cultivated land. In Belgium, the three best known are the Groenendael,

The Old English Sheepdog *(right)*, often known as the Bobtail from the tradition of docking their tails which originated in the last century when the removal of the tail made a shepherd's dog exempt from tax, is a popular breed as a pet, but he is a working dog that should be kept in the country.

The Border Collie is the most versatile and widely kept working sheepdog in the world.

the Tervuren and the Malinois. All three resemble the German Shepherd Dog although there are important differences in structure when they are examined closely.

The Australian Kelpie, developed from the Welsh sheepdogs and collies taken to Australia by the first settlers, is a fine animal, and a slight infusion of Dingo blood is said to have given it added alertness. The Australian Cattle Dog is of medium size and controls cattle by nipping at their heels. Another excellent worker is the Welsh Corgi which operates in the same way, sometimes called the 'Heeler' for this reason. There are two distinct types—the Cardigan with a long tail and the Pembroke with a very short tail. Both are well known, but the Pembroke is more often seen in Britain and the United States, where it has achieved a splendid reputation as a companion dog.

Both the Welsh Corgis, the Pembroke *(above)* and the Cardigan, were originally cattle drover's dogs. Before the advent of the railways, cattle were driven long distances from farm to slaughter house and cattle dogs were essential to move the herds. The short legs of the Corgi breeds enabled them to race in and nip the heels of recalcitrant beasts while dodging the flailing hooves. The more popular Pembroke Corgi is the smaller of the two and has a short docked tail. The Cardigan Corgi has a long tail like a fox's brush.

The versatile Border Collies *(below)* have been selected for their working abilities for many generations. The instinct to herd is inborn in most Border Collies and quite young puppies will attempt to round up any animals they come across, such as hens or ducks. Because of this built-in drive to work, they are often too highly strung to make satisfactory pets, being much happier if given a job of work to do. Highly intelligent and sensitive, the Border Collie is often used by competitors in obedience tests with great success.

The Puli *(right)* is a medium-sized Hungarian breed with a height of about 17 in. The colour and texture of the coat are unique. It always looks dull and weatherworn. Black is most common, sometimes bronzed or greying, and whole grey or white dogs are known. It is highly valued as a house dog and companion but in its homeland it was used to drive and herd sheep during the day. This is a sprightly dog with a springy gait and plenty of vigour and intelligence, which has led to the breed being used for police work in Hungary and obedience work in the States. The coat can be combed out, but the cords are a distinctive feature of the breed. The long strands of the outer coat twist round the soft, easily matted undercoat, forming a felted mass. The dog can be bathed without disturbing the corded appearance.

The black Briards *(below)* are a breed which comes from France while the slate and white Old English Sheepdog with them comes from Britain. The similarities between the two breeds indicate that they are both descended from a very old race of shaggy sheepdogs probably brought to Europe by early Asian invaders. The Briard, a long-tailed dog which can also be fawn in colour, still guards French farmsteads and has a distinguished record as an Army and Red Cross dog.

The sheepdogs of the world vary enormously in type and character each having been developed to suit the work required of it and to be at home in the terrain where it had to work. On a farm they may also serve as an all-purpose dog but even when kept as domestic pets they often display their instinctive urge to round up stragglers!

The Kelpie *(left)* is the working sheepdog of Australia where it is reckoned that one Kelpie can do the work of six men. This is a compact, tough dog capable of covering 40 to 45 miles a day. Used to dealing with vast numbers of sheep, the dogs often work out of sight of the stockmen. Where the sheep are penned in large numbers, as in the sheep sale yards, the Kelpie will run over the backs of the tightly packed flocks to reach a certain position. The Kelpie is an extremely popular breed in Australia where it is shown as well as worked, but the dog is almost unknown outside its homeland.

The Australian Cattle Dog *(above right)* is a working breed superbly adapted for a specific job—that of driving, rounding up and penning range cattle. The steers are virtually wild and the dogs have to be tough individualists prepared to bite hard and get out of the way fast. They are agile and rugged, able to work in the heat and drive herds for trips covering many hundreds of miles. They are normally blue or mottled blue in colour, probably a legacy from the Smooth Collie in their ancestry.

The Komondor *(below right)* is the largest of the sheep and cattle working dogs of Hungary and is primarily a guard dog left to watch the herds and protect them. This is a position of trust where much is left to the dog's initiative. Like many pastoral guard dogs, the Komondor is white, perhaps so that it can be seen more easily at night. The tremendous coat falls in matted cords forming an almost impenetrable mass which protects the dog against the weather and any injury. A truly impressive dog, the bigger the Komondor is the better.

Scent Hounds and Sight Hounds

Hounds fall into two categories, those that hunt by sight and those that hunt by scent. The sight hounds are the greyhounds, sometimes called the gazehounds, which have been bred for speed so that they can overtake the swiftest and most agile of quarry. They include such breeds as the Saluki, the Afghan Hound, the Borzoi or Russian Wolfhound, and the Deerhound. They have tall, elongated bodies with long powerful limbs. The back is long and arched so that it can act as a powerful spring when the dog gallops. The long strong tail acts as an efficient rudder so that the dog can turn and twist at speed. The depth of the rib cage ensures plenty of heart and lung room, and the dog carries no superfluous flesh or fat.

The dogs run mute, needing all their breath for galloping. Once its quarry is out of sight, the greyhound gives up. These dogs are therefore specifically suited to hunting in open country. They have been used on the Russian steppes to pull down wolves, in the sandy wastes of Persia to hunt gazelle and desert foxes, to hunt antelope on the plains of the Orient and deer and hares on the moors and mountainsides of Britain. As man encroaches on the open spaces of the world there is less and less for coursing hounds to hunt.

Many of these breeds are now kept solely as pets by people who admire their elegance and grace. The thrill of coursing live game across open country, which was enjoyed by so many of our ancestors, has now been replaced by the excitements of greyhound racing. This is the biggest of all modern dog businesses, and each year many thousands of dogs are registered with the appropriate governing body of the sport. Not only are winning dogs very valuable in their own right, a considerable amount of money is gambled on greyhound racing. The idea of dogs chasing a mechanically propelled artificial hare was tried out in Britain in the 1870s and failed. It was revived in the 1920s in the U.S.A. with a circular track and an electrically controlled hare. The sport very rapidly became popular throughout the States and was brought back to Britain a few years later.

The second category of hounds are those that hunt by scent. They are generally not as swift as greyhounds for they do not need to keep their quarry in sight. Following its scent they can wear the game down by persistence and endurance. These hounds are more diverse in shape than the greyhounds, and can vary from a low-legged animal like the Dachshund to a large powerful beast like the Bloodhound. They rely almost entirely on their noses for hunting and often have long pendant ears, full of folds, which hang down over the eyes when the dog is tracking. They do not run mute: the cry of the Bloodhound indicates not only the nature of the quarry but also the direction in which it is moving and how far it is ahead of the pack.

Hounds are often used by shooting men to find game and may be expected to retrieve it when it is shot. In some parts of the world, hounds are trained to work round behind game and drive it towards the guns. The greatest variety of hounds is probably to be found in France, although hunting by packs of hounds barely survived the French Revolution. In Britain the number of packs of hounds has steadily increased during the twentieth century. Most packs are foxhounds which are hunted on horseback, but there are also beagle and basset packs which are followed on foot. There are also a few trail hounds which race round the fell country in the north of England following an aniseed trail laid for them.

By far the greatest number of hounds in the modern world is in America, where there are reckoned to be well over one and a half million. Over the centuries the very best English and French hound blood has been imported into the States, although few of these dogs have been hunted in packs in the European style. The American Foxhound is used in a variety of ways and for this reason type is not very uniform. The field trial hound, which is run competitively at field trials, has to be speedy and has a rather jealous nature. The foxhound used by the sportsman who hunts the fox with a gun is a slow trailing hound with a good voice. The trail or drag hounds which race along a specially laid trail need speed and stamina alone. American Foxhounds are hunted in packs which are followed on horseback, although their quarry need not necessarily be a fox.

The Coonhound, bred to hunt racoons, is a popular American hound. When loosed at night in forest or swamp land, it casts around until it picks up a trail. It bays whilst following the scent, and when the racoon climbs a tree, remains baying at the foot of the tree until the hunter arrives.

The Afghan Hound *(right)* was known in ancient Egypt five thousand years ago. Used for coursing game in the mountainous country of Afghanistan, it is believed to be the fastest hurdler of all the hounds. They stand 27 to 29 in. high and are one of the most striking of all dogs. Their flowing long coats easily become matted and must be attended to regularly.

The Rhodesian Ridgeback *(above)* was bred by South African farmers as a guard dog and to hunt all kinds of quarry—even lions—and has the nickname 'lion dog'. They have a characteristic ridge of hair along the spine which grows in the opposite direction to the rest of the coat. A missionary is said to have taken the first dogs from the Cape to Rhodesia, where the breed was profusely bred, and so gained its name.

Foxhunting dates from about the middle of the eighteenth century, although packs of hounds have existed since man first became a hunter. Earlier hound packs hunted wild boar, wolves and deer, but as the countryside became more settled and enclosed, the larger animals of the chase became extinct and the fox, whose numbers had to be controlled, became the main object of the hunt. Packs of hounds like these English Foxhounds *(right)* have probably been bred with more care and thought over the centuries than most other animals and the result is a compact, powerful animal of tremendous stamina and scenting power.

The Pharaoh Hound *(left)* is the same type of greyhound as those depicted in the murals of ancient Egypt. The dog has a lithe, lean build and an approximately square outline when seen from the side. As well as being speedy and agile, Pharaoh Hounds are phenomenal jumpers. They are used for hunting rabbits, which they do more like a lurcher than a greyhound, for they use scent and hearing to a greater degree than sight. The large upstanding ears are a feature of the breed.

Racing Greyhounds *(above right)* are the fastest dogs in the world, reaching more than 37 miles an hour over short distances. They hunt entirely by sight and race after a mechanically propelled hare. They wear light cage-type muzzles when racing to prevent them snapping at each other in the excitement of the melee after they have crossed the finishing line.
    When it was first staged in the 1870s greyhound racing was a failure, but it became an enormous money-spinning success when revived at floodlit evening meetings in the United States and Britain during the 1920s.

All the hounds which use their keen sight to follow their quarry stem from ancient origins. The Saluki *(below right)* is also known as the Gazelle Hound because it was used to course those fleet-footed animals. There are two varieties of this breed, the feathered and the smooth, and the coat can be of any colour. They are sensitive and quiet dogs which tend to be rather withdrawn except when with the people to whom they are attached. They have a very independent nature and need plenty of exercise.

The Whippet *(left)* has aptly been described as 'one of the most graceful running machines in existence'. The breed was created in the north of England during the latter half of the nineteenth century for the sport of rabbit coursing. When this became illegal, rag racing took its place. The dogs were encouraged to swing and pull on a rag held by their owners and would race towards this entrancing object flapping at the end of the track. Today Whippets are mainly kept as pets.

The Basset Hound is another hunting dog which is better known nowadays by the fireside than in the field. Heavily boned, short-legged hounds like these were once used on the Continent to hunt everything from deer to wild boar. Modern Basset packs *(right)* hunt the hare and are followed on foot. They are known for their remarkable scenting power and perseverance, rather than their speed. As pets it should be remembered that these are large dogs on short legs which require good feeding and plenty of exercise.

The Ibizan Hound *(below)*, which is very like the Pharaoh Hound in build, comes from the little Spanish island of Ibiza, which is now such a popular holiday centre. In this and the other islands of Majorca and Minorca in the Balearics it is used to hunt rabbits, hare and partridge and trained as a gun dog to retrieve and point. Holidaymakers were attracted by its handsome looks and winning character and introduced it elsewhere. It has great agility and is extremely intelligent.

Credit for developing the ancient strains of hounds is given to St Hubert who, as a dissolute young man, placed hunting before everything. Once, hunting on Good Friday, a stag emerged before him with a fiery cross between its antlers to threaten him with hellfire if he did not observe his religious duties. He gave up his wild life and founded the Abbey of St Hubert in the Ardennes—but he continued breeding his hounds at the monastery until his death in AD 727 and his monks carried on the strain for many centuries afterwards.

The Bloodhound *(left)*, descended from St Hubert's Hounds, has the finest nose of all the hounds and can find a cold line successfully long after other breeds have given up. Their hunting skill is legendary and in the past they have been used to hunt runaway slaves, find missing persons and track down wanted criminals. Bloodhound enthusiasts still arrange hunts, a runner being sent ahead to lay a trail for the hounds to follow. The sound of their sonorous baying when following a line is said to be the most unforgettable of all hound music.

The modern Beagle *(above right)* is known in a dual role. As merry and active animals of a handy size for urban life, they are deservedly popular as pets both in the United States and Britain. As pack dogs used for hunting the hare, they have a much more ancient history. From Roman times to the modern day, Beagle packs have attracted an enthusiastic following. As they are followed on foot and not on horseback, this is an energetic sport. Part of the charm of the pet Beagle is this close sporting background.

Otterhounds *(below right)* are rather like Bloodhounds in appearance, except for their hard wiry coats, and they have the same remarkable scenting powers. They are handsome dogs, very hardy and excellent swimmers but they seem unlikely to survive in a world increasingly concerned with the conservation of the rarer wild animals, including the otter. In the United States a number of Otterhounds are exhibited at dog shows, although their numbers are relatively few. In Britain there is only one pure-bred pack and it is obviously a breed that is in grave danger of disappearing altogether.

The Norwegian Elkhound *(left)* has a claim to be one of the oldest breeds in Europe. They are dogs of endurance and stamina whose role throughout thousand of years has been to guard the home and the domestic flocks, and to co-operate with man in hunting large quarry such as bear and reindeer, as well as elk. The hounds, working alone or in pairs, were expected to locate and hold at bay these large animals until the hunters could reach the spot.

The Irish Wolfhound *(below left)* is the heavyweight and the tallest amongst the hounds. There are many references in early Irish literature to these majestic dogs, which were always highly prized and frequently sent as gifts by local chieftains. When wolves became extinct in Ireland, the Wolfhound also declined in number, only to be revived in the nineteenth century. It seems very fitting that this dignified and noble dog should be the mascot of the Irish Guards regiment.

The long, low-to-the-ground Dachshund *(right)* is a native of Germany where, as its name implies, it was bred to go underground after badgers. This dog's powerful body, supported on short legs, enabled it to enter the badger's earth and force a way through the tunnels of the badger's set until it could come to grips with the quarry or hold it at bay until it could be dug out and despatched. The dog's loud ringing bark helped the gamekeeper to locate their position underground. It is the only hound which goes to earth in the manner of a terrier, but there is no proof that any terrier blood was used in its make-up. Today Dachshunds are usually only kept as pets. They come in three different coat varieties: long-haired, smooth-haired and wire-haired. There are miniatures in all three which are very popular. Miniatures must weigh under 11 lb.

SPORTING DOGS

Many of the present-day breeds of gun dogs are descended from the sporting dogs used from medieval times to the advent of the sporting gun. Hawking was one of the favourite pastimes throughout Europe for centuries and dogs were employed to find and flush the game for the waiting hawks circling overhead. Today dogs perform the same function for the hunter with his gun.

Confusingly, early writers call all the types of sporting dogs by the name of 'spaniel'. We know, however, that different kinds of dogs were used for different functions. Springing spaniels found birds like partridge and quail and flushed them into nets. Setting spaniels or 'couchers' also used their noses to find the coveys but, instead of flushing the birds, they showed they had found game by freezing into position with head held low, one forefoot raised and tail rigidly held out behind. The aim was to try and pin the birds to the ground long enough for a movable net to be drawn over both birds and dog. In the work of the springing spaniel we can see the forerunners of the present spaniel breeds, while the setting spaniels foreshadow setters and pointers.

The earliest guns, or 'fowling peeces', were inaccurate and took a long time to come into general use. Nor was there any feeling that it was unsporting to shoot at sitting birds. Indeed so unreliable were the guns that sportsmen were advised never to fire unless it was at a group of stationary birds. As the range was so short, there was no need for a dog to collect the birds for they fell almost at the hunter's feet.

With the arrival of the breach-loading gun, the sport of shooting really began and pointers and setters came into their own. These are dogs which locate their quarry by windborne scent. They quarter the ground, ranging far ahead of the line of guns, and are lightly built, fast dogs of great stamina, which may be required to gallop across moorland all day. It was on the grouse moors of Yorkshire and Scotland that the work of pointers and setters was first seen at its best. When the dogs scent game, they freeze in the classical pose of a pointing dog, indicating the position of the birds, and try to keep them pinned down until the guns arrive. Only then, on command, do the dogs creep forward until the birds lose their nerve and fly upward, presenting a target. At the sound of the shot the dogs drop down and remain still until once more waved on to quarter the ground.

As sporting guns improved, the increased velocity meant that birds flying high overhead often fell a long way ahead of the guns. This led to the development of the retrieving breeds whose job was simply and solely to fetch back dead and wounded game. As injured birds will run great distances, retrievers had to have good noses so that they could track birds down. At first any dog that would fetch and carry game was called a 'retriever', but by 1880 all the retrieving breeds that we know today were established.

Spaniels also find and flush game but they work within the range of the gun and flush birds within that range. They flush game out of cover and are used for working through undergrowth and hedgerows, searching fields of root crops or stubble. Because this type of shooting is within the reach of the majority of shooting men, the working spaniel, in practice the English Springer, is the most widely used of modern gun dogs. Spaniels are also expected to retrieve but they are not so versatile as the final group of 'all-purpose' gun dogs. These are mainly continental breeds which are expected to find and point their birds, flush them on command and then retrieve them when they have been shot.

There is a great deal of public interest in the work of gun dogs and field trials are held in which the work of the dogs is tested competitively. These are particularly popular in America where separate trials are run for pointers and setters, for the all-purpose breeds and for retrievers. Because of the numbers involved and the enthusiasm shown, many of the conditions are artificial and the game is planted. This is in contrast to British field trials which take place under natural conditions. Although this means that these trials approximate to a normal day's shooting, it also means that one dog may be very unlucky compared with another contestant.

Urbanization is constantly restricting the amount of shooting for sport, but the interest in gun dog training is greater than ever before and field trials are becoming increasingly popular as a means of watching and comparing gun dogs at work.

The German Short-haired Pointer *(right)* is an all-purpose gun dog which will find game, point and retrieve the game when it has been flushed and shot. The German Short-haired is one of the most popular shooting dogs in America, although it only arrived in the States in the late 1920s. The toughness of the breed in facing heavy cover and its readiness to work in terrible weather conditions have won it many admirers. The breed has also been used by falconers to find game for birds of prey.

The Labrador Retriever *(left)*, both the yellow and the black, is so popular as a pet and companion that its role as a gun dog is easily forgotten. But among shooting men it is as popular as it is among pet owners. The dog's kindly nature combined with its powerful build, its excellent nose and its fondness for water, make it invaluable for retrieving game in the shooting field. Its short, glossy coat is weather- and water-resistant, and can be black, yellow or liver. Brought to England in the early nineteenth century by Labrador fishermen, the Labrador Retriever took some while to become established. Now its versatility is such that it works as a gun dog, a police dog and a guide dog for the blind, as well as being the pet of countless thousands of dog owners.

Setters are dogs trained to scent out birds and then freeze 'setting' the direction of the game for the sportsman. Rangier, and higher on the leg than the English Setter, though not so heavy as the Gordon, the Irish Setter *(right)* is nowadays almost always to be found in a rich mahogany red colour. Today most of the breed are kept as pets, their shining coats being one of their attractions. However, as sporting dogs, they are very fast and writers of a century ago remarked that they were 'slashing goers, with heads and flags well up' when they were searching for grouse on the Yorkshire moors. This is a gay dog with a headstrong, boisterous personality and it needs plenty of exercise. They were first shown in Britain in 1860 and in those days red and white Irish Setters were in the majority, the self-coloured dogs being much rarer.

The English Setter *(left)* combines great physical beauty with working ability and is one of the most widely kept bird dogs in America. The long and silky coat should be slightly wavy and the white background should be flecked and freckled with either blue, orange or lemon markings. Setters range in front of the guns in order to find game, doing exactly the same job as pointers. When they scent the birds, they freeze into a point with one foreleg held up, as if to emphasize that they have been checked in mid-stride by the odour of game.

The popularity of the English Cocker Spaniel *(right)* as a pet and companion is exceptional. It is one of the friendliest of dogs, with a merry temperament and a perpetually wagging tail, and topped the popularity poll in Britain for 20 years. Its name is supposed to have come from the breed's particular proficiency in hunting woodcock, although it is little used as a gun dog today. One of the many attractions of the breed is that it comes in so many colours.

The Flat-coated Retriever *(below)*, once the favourite companion of the Victorian shooting man and his gamekeeper, has been ousted as a gun dog by the Labrador and the Golden Retriever. The reasons for this are not obvious for the Flat-coat is a handsome and industrious dog.

The Brittany Spaniel *(left)* is a French breed now widely used, in America as well as its country of origin, as a working gun dog. This is the only spaniel breed that 'points' to indicate the presence of game. Indeed the present dog (except for its short tail) looks very like the Elizabethan 'setting spaniel', one of the ancestors of the present-day setters. Not only is it expected to find game, it will also retrieve it when shot, being an all-round gun dog rather than a specialist.

The heavyweight among the spaniels, the Clumber Spaniel *(right)*, is hardly ever worked in the field today. This seems to be not so much because its working abilities have declined but because the style of shooting has changed. Such a dignified, heavyweight dog is of necessity a slow worker. Pushing through dense undergrowth with stubborn tenacity, the Clumber overlooks nothing in the way of game, and its stately progress through the coverts suited overweight or ageing Edwardian sportsmen. Modern shooting moves at a faster pace and the virtues of the Clumber have been forgotten.

Early documents suggest that a Welsh spaniel may have been known as early as AD 300. The name Welsh Springer *(below left)* did not come into use until 1902 but the dog's distinctive colouring of gleaming ice-white and brilliant chestnut red makes it easily identifiable in prints and paintings throughout the centuries. They are not, and never have been, a fashionable breed but they are in little danger of dying out as they are appreciated as general-purpose working animals in their home country. They are vigorous, keen hunters with hardy constitutions, but they also make gentle house dogs.

Early writers divided sporting dogs into land spaniels and water spaniels. Sixteenth-century pictures of water spaniels show them to have long low-set ears and thick curly coats—their modern descendants include the Poodle and the Irish Water Spaniel —but other gun dogs will often work well in water like this English Setter *(right)*.

The Chesapeake Bay Retriever *(above)* is an American breed which has never achieved the popularity its reputation might suggest. It is one of a number of breeds whose speciality is retrieving wildfowl from water, especially wild duck. One of the remarkable features of the breed is its coarse, oily coat which helps it to shed water and ice simply by a good shake.

Many of the German sporting breeds
were decimated in the two World
Wars, although the same dogs have
often been taken back to their own
homeland by returning servicemen,
the breeds thus beginning a new life
in a different area of the world. The
Large Munsterlander *(left)*, the
descendant of the ancient German
Long-haired Pointer, is still few in
number. A handful of pure-bred dogs
of this type were preserved in
Munsterland and are now well
established in Germany and beginning
to be known in Britain. The colouring
is the traditional one for this breed,
white with black patches and black
ticking.

The Curly-coated Retriever *(right)* is
the oldest and the oddest of the
retrieving breeds. The tight curls of
its coat come from the water spaniel
and suggest the breed's speciality is
retrieving on marsh and saltflats and
in river estuaries. After its Victorian
heyday, it has always been a minority
breed, kept going by a handful of
enthusiasts. The Curly-coated Retriever
has been used to retrieve duck and
quail in Australia and New Zealand
and has always been admired as a
tender-mouthed and steady dog.
Recently in Britain several have
been trained as guide dogs for the
blind because of their patient and
reliable temperament.

The Irish Water Spaniel *(below left)*
is often called the clown of the spaniel
family because of the contrast
between its curly topknot and smooth
face. It is always a rich liver colour
and the coat should have crisp, tight
ringlets with a natural oiliness. This is
a dog with a different look but it has
never caught the public fancy and its
numbers are dangerously low.

As there is an Irish Setter and an
English Setter, the black-and-tan
Gordon Setter *(below right)* should
really have been called the Scottish
one. It is a bigger, more raw-boned
dog than the other two and a
methodical, dependable worker with a
great deal of stamina in the field. It is
mentioned by a Scottish writer in
the seventeenth century as the 'black
and fallow setting dog', but it was
really the Fourth Duke of Richmond
and Gordon who perfected the breed
in the early 1800s. Most Gordons today
are pets and show dogs.

The Vizsla (below) is a multi-purpose gun dog from Hungary which points game, marks the fall of the dead bird and then retrieves it on command. In Hungary the dog is expected to work equally well whether the guns are after hares, francolin, partridge, ducks or geese. For this reason it is taught to search fairly close to the hunter on foot and not to range in the way of the English pointer.

The Pointer (above right) is valued for its working qualities in every part of the world where people are interested in shooting game. It ranges from side to side ahead of the guns, searching for the elusive scent of the game with its extraordinarily sensitive nose. Once it has found the scent, the dog freezes like a statue, literally pointing the way. With head held high, foreleg raised as though in the act of taking a step and tail held rigid in the air, the dog will remain motionless, as if entranced, for as long as it takes the sportsmen to come up behind.

The English breeds of gun dog are usually worked only as pointers or retrievers and many shooting parties will take out a dog of each kind. On the Continent and in North America such breeds as the Weimaraner (below right) are trained to carry out both tasks. Most European countries produced their own version of the Pointer and this breed was one of those evolved in Germany. It is a striking-looking dog which is sometimes known as the 'grey ghost dog' as it is always mouse brown or silver grey in colour, usually with beautiful topaz or amber eyes. The breed was produced by the sportsmen nobles at the court of Weimar and later protected by a German breed club which strictly controlled breeding and ownership. An American sportsman who was admitted to this exclusive club took the breed to the States where it became an enormous success, as much as an obedience trials dog and companion as a gun dog.

GUARDS, GUIDES AND RESCUE DOGS

There are so many ways in which the dog has helped and served man. For centuries he was an actual combatant on the field of battle. War dogs were used by the Assyrians and Babylonians, and the invading Romans were much impressed by the fighting strength of the British Mastiff. Early Irish literature mentions that Wolfhounds accompanied their masters into battle and were large and strong enough to pull the enemy from his horse. Modern Army and Air Force dogs no longer have this offensive role; instead they are used in the role of communications. They lay telephone cables and carry messages, being trained to run to and fro between two masters. Army dogs are used for mine detection as they can scent buried mines from a distance. Trained mine-detecting dogs save both time and manpower. The Air Force uses trained dogs to find the missing parts of crashed planes. Air Force dogs are also used as the most efficient way of guarding aerodromes. The dogs' acute hearing and their ability to pick up windborne scents mean that they can detect intruders hundreds of yards away. When they detect an intruder on an airfield, they may be loosed to detain the trespasser until the arrival of their handler. Army patrol dogs, however, which are used in guerrilla warfare to detect the presence of the enemy, must not give away their position by approaching a suspected ambush or by barking or growling. When they pick up an alien scent that may indicate danger, they are trained to freeze or point like a gun dog scenting game. During the Second World War, rescue dogs were parachuted down with stretcher bearers of the airborne divisions.

Many villages in the Middle Ages kept a bloodhound to track down marauders and thieves, but the first real police dogs were recruited in 1859 by the Ghent police. These were so successful that the German authorities experimented with a kennel based in Brunswick, and other districts followed suit until, by 1910, the dogs were attached to all police forces on a permanent basis.

A trained police dog doubles the efficiency of the patrol man. All policemen are taught to observe closely but a dog has the added advantage of keener hearing and amazing powers of scent—senses which are not affected by darkness. It is obvious that a criminal has far less chance of escape once he has been detected by the dog. Furthermore, a policeman attacked by hooligans may be seriously injured if on his own—a dog will instil fear into his attackers and break up the mob until help arrives. Another important part of a police dog's training is tracking, and German Shepherds and Dobermans are efficient and quick workers and are scientifically trained to arrest a man without intentional injury. The dogs are taught to seize a man by the sleeve of his jacket, attempting to throw him off balance, and will hold onto an armed criminal even if they have been wounded. Police dogs are not always after criminals, they are employed frequently by security firms as guard dogs, and are used to find missing persons and lost property.

The dog's scenting powers have been used in many ways. The Italians still use dogs to hunt truffles, those elusive and expensive underground fungi. Gas companies use dogs to search for gas leaks, thus saving the expense of digging up a whole pipeline. Police and customs' dogs are trained to search for drugs.

In all mountainous areas in the world dogs are employed to rescue people lost or hurt or buried in the snow after an avalanche. The Austrian Mountain Rescue Service is one of the most efficient and the breeds used are German Shepherd Dogs and Belgian Sheepdogs, as both have the intelligence, stamina, and thick inner and outer coats necessary for working in Arctic conditions. Also, animals with dark coats are less vulnerable to the ultra-violet rays found at great heights which can affect their eyes. It is necessary to apply an anti-freeze mixture to their coats to avoid the snow sticking to the hair and thus hindering their work.

The men of the Avalanche Rescue Service must also be tough, experienced mountaineers with a thorough understanding of dog nature. Training of the puppies starts at twelve months with a grounding of general obedience, and is followed by jumping, both high and low, and the finding of objects hidden in long grass to encourage nose work. The dogs are worked over very rough ground and taken in every variety of transport so that nothing will be strange to them. The advanced training is very complicated and far too long to explain here. The dog is taught to find first his master who is buried in a simulated grave of varying depths and at increasing distances away, and then a stranger in the same way, until he is ready for work in the snow. They find avalanche casualties by scent, and can detect victims buried under several feet of snow. Their work is invaluable, as men are virtually helpless in such conditions.

Dogs have been used extensively as pack animals. The explorer Marco Polo remarked on the sledges drawn by mastiff-like dogs in Manchuria, and sledge dogs once provided the only means of transport for all the peoples inhabiting the frozen wastes of Alaska, Greenland and Siberia. These dogs endured lives of

The German Shepherd Dog (right) is an extremely versatile working dog and has been employed as a guide, guard, police, rescue and search dog as well as in his original shepherd role.

The Arctic Sled Dog (left), for so long the only means of transport in that region, must be among the toughest of all working animals. The Eskimos use them for haulage and hunting, for warmth and for food when times are very bad. The dogs are accustomed to feeding on frozen scraps and to sleeping in hollows which they scrape in the frozen surface of the tundra. Blizzards often cover them with drifted snow but, insulated by their thick coats, they can sleep out the worst of storms. Various methods of harnessing are used but the most popular is couples of dogs fastened on either side of a trace going out to the team leader.

That canine giant the St Bernard (right) is one of the ten most popular breeds in the United States. These dogs are associated with legendary feats of rescue, finding and guiding to safety travellers lost in the snowdrifts of the St Bernard Pass across the Alps. Although mountain rescues still take place, the work is now done by the lighter and more versatile German Shepherd. The benevolent and kindly disposition of the St Bernard, plus its impressive size, ensures the dog a host of admirers.

incredible hardship, for, although they were highly valued and well looked after by their owners, the conditions under which they lived and worked were such that only the fittest and toughest could survive. Farm dogs in Europe were once used as draught dogs, pulling loads of bread, cork, olives, wine, baskets and cheeses. Pack dogs carrying food and ammunition have accompanied hunters in the field and dogs took shells forward to the guns in the First World War. Today draught dogs are dimishing rapidly in numbers every-

where in the world as their role is taken over by the internal combustion engine. But as one kind of work disappears dogs become useful in other ways, for instance, in medical and space research or for guiding the blind.

The working dog has come a long way from the wolf-dog which hunted with our ancestors, and the end is not yet. There is still a place for our dogs in spite of the mechanical and electronic marvels which are constantly being invented.

As Eskimo settlements are invariably isolated, a number of distinct types of husky were evolved. Many of these breeds were lost during the Alaska gold rush when every dog, whatever its shape and size, was pressed into service to haul prospectors and their supplies to the gold fields. One breed that did survive was the Siberian Husky *(left)*. This is a comparatively lightweight haulage dog, well known through the popularity of the sport of sled dog racing. Many Siberians are shown and kept as companions, and they adapt well to a temperate climate. The light blue eyes are quite common in this breed.

One of the largest and heaviest of all breeds, the Mastiff *(right)* was also one of Britain's first exports. The invading Romans, under the leadership of Julius Caesar, were so impressed by the British dogs fighting alongside their masters that they sent some to Rome to take part in the gladiatorial games. Sadly, breeding stock in Britain did not survive the Second World War and Mastiffs would have become extinct in their native land had American owners not supplied further specimens. This must be the most impressive of guard dogs for those with the money for its upkeep.

Dogs of Spitz type *(below right)* are the working dogs of the northern latitudes. This group of dogs all have wedge-shaped heads with blunt powerful jaws and small pricked ears. The bushy tail is usually curled up over the back and the dense coat offers a complete protection against the harshest winter weather. All the sled dogs are of this type and so are a number of other northern breeds. This Norwegian farm dog suckles her litter in between her work, which can be anything from driving the cows out to pasture, accompanying the farmer out shooting or guarding the farmyard against human or animal intruders.

The British Bulldog *(left)* is the national symbol of tenacity and courage, both of which were needed in the days when the dog was used for bull-baiting. Once bull-baiting became illegal, the dog changed both its shape and its character. Now the massive scowling head masks a gentle and affectionate nature and its cumbersome shape implies that the Bulldog prefers a comfortable, amiable way of life to the rigours of its past existence. Both modern Bulldogs and modern bulls have become muscle-bound leviathans, very different from the days when they were pitted against each other.

The Pyrenean Mountain Dog or Great Pyrenées *(above right)* used to guard flocks of sheep from wolves and other predators in the isolated mountain areas of France. By the seventeenth century it had become a fashionable dog in aristocratic French circles and guarded many of the chateaux of south-west France. The beautiful coat and impressive size make the Pyrenean a very attractive dog, but it needs adequate space, a great deal of food, and time spent on daily grooming if it is to be seen at its best.

It seems odd that so popular and well known a dog as the Boxer *(below right)* should have such a comparatively short history. The breed is a German one, developed from dogs of the bulldog and mastiff types which were used for bull-baiting and dogfighting. Energy and courage are characteristics still possessed by the modern Boxer, a breed which makes a devoted companion and guard. The Boxer was one of the first breeds used for police work in Germany but did not become popular in Britain or America until the late 1940s.

The Labrador Retriever *(overleaf)* is widely used as a guide dog and in police work. Guiding the blind is one of the most responsible jobs a dog can have and one which no other animal can perform. Guide dogs need not be of any particular breed but should be of medium size as the giant breeds are too big for comfortable working and too costly to maintain. They should have a stable temperament, neither nervous nor aggressive. They must be willing to please and have a high degree of concentration. In practice Labradors and Golden Retrievers are the most common breeds

chosen for this work. German Shepherds and even a pure-bred Malamute have been used, while numbers of cross-bred bitches are taken in every year and give long and faithful service. The animals are obtained by gift, purchase, or are bred at the Centres, and it is their temperament that is all important. There must be no trace of nervousness, and the dog must be friendly, but not the type which fawns upon strangers. It must pay intelligent attention to the human voice, use its own initiative, and not show aggression towards other animals. Like Foxhounds, the puppies are 'walked' by volunteers from twelve weeks to ten months of age, and these temporary owners are expected to housetrain the pups, and familiarize them with traffic and riding in buses and trains. Training takes from four to six months and Guide Dog trainers are highly skilled and professional men and women who teach the dog to allow for the size of his master wherever they go,

and to be aware of traffic. The dog is then matched to his prospective owner who must also be taught how to co-operate and care for the dog. This takes a month, by which time the two are usually perfectly in harmony physically and mentally for their new life.

The Labrador is also the latest recruit in the battle against drug smuggling (*previous pages, right*). Police officers and customs officials are beginning to appreciate the worth of a trained dog whose nose can find hidden cargoes which might be missed even after a laborious and time-consuming search. It takes some months to train a dog in drug detection and such an animal is considered a specialist and relieved from other police duties. Drugs can be detected by the dogs even when in closed, sealed canisters. This yellow Labrador is searching for cannabis.

The highly-trained dogs of the Royal Air Force (*below*) show off their skills to the public at Air Force displays but woebetide any trespasser who should meet this German Shepherd Dog on the airfield perimeter.

The German Shepherd is also the dog most widely used by police forces throughout the world (*right*). Their high degree of trainability plus their agility and strength make them an ideal choice as police and Army dogs. Attacking on command is only one of the many facets of the work they are trained for, although it is probably the one with the most news value. Police work demands reliability and steadiness of nerve and a well-trained German Shepherd has both. Because they are very intelligent, they are happiest as working companions and can become dangerously aggressive if allowed to get bored. In England, police dogs live at home with their trainers as part of the family so that a complete relationship can be established.

TERRIERS

The dog is basically a hunting animal and the hunting breeds are by no means limited to the hounds. While the hounds have been bred selectively to develop their ability to chase and overcome their quarry, a different group of breeds have been developed to dig out animals that have gone to earth and to control rodent populations. These are the terriers, which come in a tremendous variety of shapes, colours, sizes and coat textures and which have a history probably as long as that of the hounds.

In the fifteenth century Dame Juliana Berners, the Prioress of an English nunnery, wrote a book—perhaps a little surprisingly for a churchwoman—on the subject of hunting, in which she classified the 'Teroures' as a breed used in field sports. In 1576 John Caius, physician to Queen Elizabeth I, wrote a treatise on English dogs in which he also mentions 'Terrarius or Terrars' as 'dogges serving the pastime of hunting beasts'. He went on to say that their work caused them to creep underground in pursuit of foxes and badgers. In fact this is how they get their name for, although they may strike terror in the heart of the animals they hunt, it is the latin word *terra*: ground, from which terrier comes.

The twentieth-century terriers that bolt foxes and rabbits and kill rats are doing the same work as their ancestors and they have the same courageous and tenacious characters. Their fighting instincts led to breeds being developed as fighting dogs, either to bait other animals or to battle with each other, crosses being made with the bigger mastiff breeds which had provided the war dogs of ancient times.

Terriers can be extremely versatile, for instance an Airedale won the first American Police Dog Trials in Madison Square Garden. In fact this breed, which carries Otterhound blood, was expert at catching water rats and has been used as an all-round sportsman, even hunting water buck and boar, but does not go to ground for it is too large. There are one or two other large breeds in the group which, although they have all the terrier character, fail to live up to their name in this way.

A typical terrier needs a good strong voice so that it can keep in touch with the huntsmen when it is working. Once a terrier has marked its quarry underground it should keep on barking to let the men on the surface know its whereabouts. They can then dig down and come to grips with the fox or badger. A silent dog can easily be lost or injured underground and never heard of again. The tendency of the smaller terriers to enjoy the sound of their own voices is not, however, always appreciated by owners today, who no longer want to work them.

The terrier group have become popular household pets and come in both smooth and rough varieties. Although it is difficult to trace the ancestry of the latter, they have been around for many centuries. As terriers have been developed as pets, and for the show ring, special trims and clips have become customary for certain breeds and it should always be remembered that the longer-haired dog will need more careful grooming. Nevertheless, however much the terrier is removed from his original work he will probably still be quite a fighter. He may need strong handling but he will make an excellent guard and a loyal companion.

The Sealyham (below left) was created a century ago in Wales but the Bedlington Terrier (above) is an older terrier breed and has been known in the Northumberland district of Britain since the early 1800s. Often called the Gypsy Dog, the Bedlington was the poacher's partner, for the breed combined the vermin-killing instincts of the terrier with the speed of a hound like the whippet. Trimming emphasizes the dog's distinctive outline, and its lamb-like appearance is heightened by the unique

flaxen of the coat and the fact that most Bedlingtons are blue in colour, although liver and sandy are also acceptable.

The West Highland White (below) is now the most popular terrier in Britain, probably because they are very natural dogs, with a light-hearted and plucky temperament. They come from the same root as Scottish Terriers and Cairn Terriers and although their coat is white it is harsh in texture and easily sheds dirt.

The Boston Terrier *(above)* was bred in the 1870s, in the town it was named after, for pit fighting and was probably developed from crossing Bulldogs and Bull Terriers. Sometimes called 'the perfect American gentleman' it no longer displays an aggressive spirit but is still well able to take care of itself if necessary.

The Australian Terrier *(left)*, created in Melbourne in 1885, is one of the smallest working terriers. It is a sensible-sized dog for those living in flats and small maisonettes and its spirit and air of assurance make it an excellent housedog.

The Jack Russell Terrier *(above right)* is not an officially recognized breed but is firmly established as a pet in Britain. It is named for a Devon vicar but today's dogs probably bear little resemblance to those which he originally bred in the nineteenth century.

The Lakeland Terrier *(below right)* comes from the fell country of northern England where it accompanied the packs of fell hounds and went to ground after foxes. It has a well-balanced head with powerful jaws, and its narrow body enables it to wriggle through rock fissures and crannies. The modern show dog has the dense wiry coat thinned out to smarten its appearance but at heart it is still a game working dog.

The Smooth Fox Terrier *(left)* has never been out of fashion, unlike its cousin the Wire-haired Fox Terrier *(right)*, whose much-barbered look may have something to do with its present decline from popularity. The difference between the two lies in coat rather than structure and in the nineteenth century, when most were still kept for killing stable rats, they were bred together indiscriminately. Fox Terriers also used to run with the hounds and came into their own when the fox went to earth.

The Cairn Terrier *(below)* is a Scottish breed which lacks a well-documented history. It was used in western Scotland to tackle all vermin from rats to wild cats and therefore did not move in the sort of company where its history was likely to be written down. A cheeky little dog with a shaggy coat that needs little in the way of attention, the Cairn is one of the most popular terriers in Britain and well established in America, Australia and on the Continent. Its gay and lively disposition makes it a cheerful companion.

COMPANION DOGS

There are many dogs which today we do not think of in a working role, whatever the original reason for their development, and there are others, which, from the first, have been developed entirely as domestic pets. Although the earliest records of dogs usually show them in a hunting or fighting capacity the lapdog had already found itself a priveleged place in ancient times.

One pet, called Issa, which belonged to the Roman Governor of Malta in the time of Christ, was obviously as petted and pampered as any lapdog since. She was described by a contemporary poet as 'More frolicsome than Catulla's sparrow, purer than a dove's kiss, gentler than a maiden and more precious than Indian gems. Lest the last days that she sees the light should snatch her from him for ever Publius has had her painted.' The painting has not survived so we do not know whether she was of the same type as the modern Maltese breed, but very similar dogs appear among some of the earliest representations of pets. They were very popular fifteen centuries later in the time of Elizabeth I when Dr. Caius wrote: 'They are very small indeed and chiefly sought after for the pleasure and amusement of women who carry them in their arms, their bosoms and their beds.'

Not all modern companion dogs are small. There are quite large breeds, such as the Chow Chow, which were hard working dogs in their original homes but have never been expected to earn their living in most countries where they are now known. Others were bred to perform tasks which are no longer part of contemporary life. Some are small successors to a once larger breed. The Pomeranian, for instance, was originally a much larger, spitz-type herding dog, big enough to be used to pull a cart, but occasional small puppies that appeared in litters caught the interest of some breeders. They were often disposed of as runts, but those who reared them found that although small they did not grow up to be stunted dwarfs but perfect, absolutely normal miniatures of the breed. By Queen Victoria's time they were being produced at an adult weight of between 12 and 16 lb, already much smaller than the original 'small' puppies had been when grown, and the Queen's dogs of this weight became the accepted type. However, during her reign miniaturization went further and the Queen's dogs were soon considered giants. Today the standard for this breed requires a weight of not more than $5\frac{1}{2}$ lb and something closer to 4 lb is more usual among champion dogs.

The large type of Pomeranian is no longer known, but in many cases a miniature breed exists alongside a standard size and sometimes, as in the Schnauzer, there may even be three different sizes recognized.

Little dogs have just as much need of exercise and a healthy diet as any other dogs. They should not be crammed with sweets, over-pampered or their natural life restricted just to keep them looking pretty. Like any of the larger breeds of dog they need the freedom to run and romp—even if they do get mud on their beautifully groomed and spotless coats.

The Chihuahua (left) is the smallest dog in the world and can weigh as little as 1 lb, although 4–5 lb is a more realistic weight. This little dog, in spite of its size, is both robust and hardy. The smooth-coated Chihuahua has always been the favourite but the long-coated dog is rapidly catching up.

The Chow Chow (above right) is no miniature but although in its Chinese homeland it served many roles, among them draught dog, gun dog and even table delicacy, it is known in the west as a companion dog. Although an independent personality who likes to go pioneering entirely by himself it is ideal for people living alone for it is intensely loyal to its owner and shows very little interest in other people. The characteristics of the breed include the rather scowling face, a bluish-black tongue which is unique in dogdom, and an almost straight hind leg.

The Dalmatian (below right) must have a claim as the dog with the most nicknames, being affectionately known as the 'plum pudding dog', the 'spotted Dick' and the 'fire-house dog'. The Dalmatian first became popular as a carriage dog. As well as destroying stable rats, it trotted out with the horses and, as a smart accessory, lent a final air of distinction to a gentleman's equipage.

The King Charles Spaniel *(left)* or English Toy Spaniel is a short-faced toy breed which was more popular in late Victorian times than it is today. This breed has always been divided into four different colour varieties, each distinct enough to have its own name and history. These are the Prince Charles, which is a tricolour of white, black and tan; the Ruby, a chestnut red; the Blenheim, white and red; and the black and tan. The popularity of the larger Cavalier has quite eclipsed the King Charles, which is in danger of disappearing altogether.

The Australian Silky Terrier *(below)*, also known as the Sydney Silky, was created by crossing the Australian and Yorkshire Terriers with a dash of Skye Terrier in the background somewhere. It is larger than the Yorkie and not so aggressive as the Australian Terrier but shows courage and intelligence.

The exotic Papillon *(left)* is said to have hailed originally from Mexico. These sweet-natured dogs should not be unduly small, the ideal height at withers being 8 to 11 in.

The diminutive Yorkshire Terrier *(right)* will grow up to 8 in. tall and weigh up to 7 lb. The short fluffy coat will grow to floor length, and be a dark steel blue and tan colour with a fine silky texture. If the dog is a show dog, its owner will be constantly preoccupied with protecting its coat. A pet 'Yorkie' often leads a life more suited to its natural character for, although many lead very pampered lives, they are spirited dogs which like to rush about in true terrier fashion, if given half a chance. The Yorkshire Terrier is the most popular toy dog in Britain.

The Pug *(below)* first came to Britain from Holland. It was very fashionable in the mid-Victorian era when every lady of note felt she had to own one. The earliest Pugs were fawn with a black mask, and the first all-black Pug was not shown until 1886. When the adjective 'Victorian' became synonymous with 'old-fashioned', the Pug also fell out of favour. Today there is a revival and the Pug once again has a host of admirers. They are thickset, compact dogs which do not require coddling. They are alert and playful but a watch needs to be kept on their waistline as a fat Pug is an abomination.

The hairless dogs have always been amongst the rarest and most bizarre of breeds. The only one to have made any real headway is the Chinese Crested *(left)*, which is now exhibited regularly in Britain. Except for the plume of hair on the tail and the crest on the head, the dog is naked. The skin colour varies, but it is usually mottled like the bark of a plane tree. The reason for the hairlessness is not known and, without the protection afforded by a coat of hair, the Chinese Crested has to be guarded against sunburn as well as extremes of cold.

The Pekingese *(below)* is one of the oldest breeds although it did not reach the West until about a century ago. Known in China as 'Lion Dogs' they were bred to frighten away evil spirits and ownership was restricted to those of royal blood.

The Maltese *(right)* is Europe's oldest breed of lapdog and has been known from as far back as Roman times. Its coat requires a great deal of attention but its high spirits and good nature make it a popular pet.

The Shih Tzu *(far right)* is a very recent breed in the West but has long been known in China and originally came from Tibet. It too needs careful grooming every day.

The Pomeranian *(above)* is actually descended from German cattle dogs and dogs used to round up reindeer but long ago this dwarf version of the Spitz type was well established as a lapdog and often appears in art of the past centuries, including canvases by Gainsborough. Queen Victoria owned a kennel of Poms and it was said to be her favourite dog.

The Japanese Spaniel *(below)*, despite its name, actually originated in China and probably got this name because one was given as a present to the Mikado of Japan. Over a century ago a pair was sent to the Austrian Emperor. Such royal dogs have a suitably regal bearing, like that of the Pekingese, but their higher leg gives them a more sprightly appearance.

The Brussels Griffon *(right)* is a toy dog which is small in size but big in personality. The hansom cab drivers of Brussels had small rough-haired dogs which rode importantly on the front seat of the hansom when their masters were working and caught the rats in the stable in their off-duty hours. The gamin charm of these dogs attracted attention and, modified by crossing with various other breeds, the Brussels Griffon was born. They are sturdy little dogs, built like cobs, and full of a sense of their own importance. There are two varieties of coat, rough and smooth.

The French Bulldog (*right*) is a sweet-tempered and affectionate pet which does not demand a great deal of exercise or grooming. When it was first brought to England from France in the late 1890s it was the centre of a great deal of controversy. Die-hards maintained that the Bulldog was so British a breed that even the thought of a French Bulldog was impossible. However, not only did they exist, they also flourished, particularly in America. It was in the States that the very distinctive upright bat ear was securely established as a breed characteristic. Robust and active, the French Bulldog is a much less exaggerated shape than its English counterpart. The smooth coat can be brindle, fawn or pied.

LOOKING AFTER YOUR DOG

Do not be disappointed if the bold puppy you collected at the kennel is suddenly overcome by all the strange sights and noises of his new home, and goes all shy. A few soothing words and a small meal will soon bring him round again. One of the best ways to reassure him is to sit down on the floor and let him come to you. If he has disappeared under a chair, do *not* try to drag him out as this will only scare him. Have patience and let him come out by himself, and use your voice a lot. So many owners do not talk to their dogs, and a small puppy will get great comfort from you if you encourage him in this way.

The best bed for a puppy of the small breeds is a small wooden box turned on its side, with a small piece of wood tacked across the front to keep his cushion or blanket from falling out. This is much more comforting than the open basket which most people tend to buy. It is also useful in training him to stay at home alone, as it can be turned with the opening at the top so that his blanket or bed is at the bottom, and he cannot then get out unaided. Give him a hot water bottle wrapped in a bag or a piece of blanket. This will help to console him for the loss of his brothers and sisters. Of course he will protest at first and some will take longer than others to accept being alone. Do not be tempted to lift him out. You may decide he is to sleep in your bedroom, in which case still stick to the box routine. If you think he wants to go out to attend to the calls of nature, take him out and if he obliges be sure to praise him. In this way the basis of his housetraining will be laid. Of course no small puppy can go right through the night without making a puddle. Therefore if he cries in the night, have some newspaper laid down near his box and encourage him to use it. Many flat owners who have

pets train their dogs in this way. However, if you are lucky enough to have a garden, try and train him to go outside as soon as possible.

It is most important that you put him out frequently —always first thing in the morning and last thing at night, *always* after food, and if he has been asleep during the day, hurry him out as soon as he wakes up. It is better to prevent him making his 'mistakes' rather than correcting him afterwards. Try to arrange his arrival when you yourself are free to devote some time to him each day. He will have to learn to stay alone sometimes, so start off with short periods at first; if he barks, go back to him, saying 'No' in a firm tone and put him in his bed. Give him some toys such as the hard rubber bones sold at the pet stores, rather than anything soft that he can chew to pieces. His teeth can be very sharp and bits of rubber are certainly not good for him.

These stores also sell Beef Chewy Sticks, which are excellent toys, and it does not matter if he eats them up in time. They are made of cow hide and cannot hurt him, and what is more will keep him happy and help his teething. The bigger breeds can soon make short work of them, so a large marrow bone can replace these. Be sure it is a marrow bone and not the kind that can splinter; examine it well to ensure there are no sharp pieces which are loose that he can swallow. Many owners give their puppies bones with no dire results and they are lulled into a false security thinking 'Bones don't hurt my puppy.' Then one day one gets stuck and the result can be fatal, or at best there has to be an operation to remove it, so do not chance it.

While on the subject of foreign bodies, puppies are very prone to pick up and swallow stones, coal etc. If your puppy does eat something on no account give him

Puppies like these young Beagles *(left)* need space to run and play or they will not develop as well as they should. Puppies kept in minute pens under insanitary conditions cannot follow their instincts to keep their bed and immediate surroundings clean, and this can lead to housetraining problems later.

Most dogs, like most children, like to show off and this Poodle *(above right)* is no exception. Teaching your dog games and tricks will give you both a lot of fun. Use the dog's natural abilities to the full, for example, teaching it to use its nose to search for hidden objects, and develop tricks from things your dog does naturally. Some small dogs quite often walk on their hind legs when they want to see higher and further.

castor oil. Always keep in the house a bottle of liquid paraffin which is a soothing lubricant. One or two teaspoons of this, according to the age and size of the dog, will help him pass what he has swallowed.

If your puppy has not been inoculated, this is the first thing you must arrange. On no account let him come in contact with any other dogs until after this has been done. It is absolutely essential. *Do not* put it off— you may bring disease from other animals in to him on your shoes or clothes. He has a certain immunity from his mother against all diseases, but this only lasts up to about six to seven weeks. From that time he is extremely vulnerable, and a small puppy has very little resistance. The vaccination will protect him against all the four serious diseases to which any puppy is prone. These are Distemper, or Hard Pad, Virus Hepatitis, which is a killer and can be effective in a very short time, Leptospirosis Canicola, which attacks dogs living in towns and is also a killer, and finally an equally virulent one, Leptospirosis Icterohaemorrhagiae, which is carried by rats which the country dog comes in contact with.

Do not delay, do it today should be your slogan throughout your dog's life. If at any time he shows any sign of illness, or refuses food for more than a day do not force food on him. A cold nose is not always an indication of good health. If he seems dull or out of sorts, phone your vet. He will not blame you if it is only a passing ailment, as he would much rather see a puppy at the very start of its illness and so have a better chance of a cure, than be faced with one already seriously ill. Baby puppies can go down hill very quickly. When obtaining a new puppy make sure he has been wormed. This very necessary dosing should have been done at least once or twice before you have him. Most puppies have these pests, and older dogs pick them up occasionally, but they are easily cured. Your vet will give you some pills that cause no discomfort and cost no more

than the ones advertized by the pet stores, and his dose will be correctly matched to the size and age of the dog.

You may see roundworms in a puppy's motions. They are white and about 3 in. long. An older dog may get tapeworms. There are pills for both kinds.

Fresh water should always be available for all dogs. *Always* leave a bowl down in the same place all day and every day. A distended stomach after food and a loss of shine on the coat may both indicate worms.

A dog does not require collar and lead exercise before the age of four months but you can get a puppy used to them both while walking round your garden. Do not use a harness. Let him get used to a small rounded collar first of all, then attach the lead and let him trail it along. Finally pick it up and try and go with him so that he does not feel the pull of it. When he does he will probably plunge about but by having patience and giving a short lesson every day he will soon learn it does not hurt and by the time he is ready for walks he will be used to it.

When you have got him lead trained, but not before he is at least four months old, take him for a road walk of up to about 20 minutes. Take him in a quiet road at first until he is used to the odd car, though by now he should be car-trained if you have been taking him out with you. As he gets older increase the distance and when you think he is quite nerve free and unmoved by noises, take him into the shops with you. This is particularly valuable if you want to show him later on.

From six to eight months of age onwards, he should have regular road exercise, especially if he is going to grow large. About 30 to 40 minutes should be about right. He should also have a free galloping period, either in a large paddock or out with you in the fields. Do not overdo this with the big hounds and do give him regular rest periods every day. Shut him away where he has to sleep and cannot jump up at every noise he hears. A good time for this is after his mid-day meal, and at least two hours is a good idea. He will of course sleep at other times during the day, but this set rest period should be a part of his training. Greyhound trainers always do this and the hounds are put away where there is not even a window that they can jump up at to look out. This may not be so important for a little dog, but it is a must for those who will grow to be 22 in. or more when they are adult.

Quite a good way to exercise the big hounds is to put them on a lead and take them out with a bicycle. This must be with a responsible person who will not run him too fast. The pace must only be a brisk trot or fast walk and he must not go before he is eight to nine months old. This will help greatly to strengthen his hindquarters and back muscles. A weakness in these regions is often the cause of bad action in the show ring.

Do not take him on any long walks if he shows any weakness or signs of rickets in his front legs; you will

Overfeeding and lack of exercise are evident in all too many domestic pets and the overweight that results can lead to a number of health hazards for the unfortunate dogs concerned. Owners should not let their animals run these risks for it is their fault entirely if the dog is given too much food and not taken out for sufficient exercise. You do not have to stretch your legs as vigorously as your dog does if you can teach him games which give him extra exercise—although a brisk walk for a few miles every day would do most of us some good.

This Golden Retriever *(left)* is energetically keeping fit without over-exhausting its owner and thoroughly enjoying itself. The breed is good tempered and their kindly nature makes them ideal as friends and companions to young children.

Digging a hole, or investigating one that someone else has dug, is one of the pleasures of a dog's life, especially for a Jack Russell Terrier *(right)* which comes from stock specially bred for digging out animals and investigating burrows. Nevertheless when you are out for a walk a well trained and disciplined dog should leave its rabbiting and other explorations and come straight to heel at your command. When a dog buries a bone, or some other treasured object, it is most unlikely to imply that the dog, squirrel-like, is storing food for future times of shortage—in fact bones have little or no nutritional value, although gnawing them will give the gums excellent exercise and the dog considerable pleasure. The cache is much more a way of keeping the dog's property private and out of the jaws and paws of others.

notice this if he stands badly in front.

Coat care. A dog should be groomed from puppyhood to get him used to being handled and standing still and doing as he is told. Grooming is as good a way of teaching him as any. Unless he is one of the very large breeds, stand him on a table, making sure it is not a slippery surface and does not wobble about. Place your hand gently on his hindquarters and the other on his head, at the same time saying his name and the command 'sit'. Then proceed to brush and comb him.

A bristle or nylon and bristle brush is as good as any for all puppies except perhaps the very fine smooth coated ones, when a softer kind may be used. If he tries to jump down, as he very well may, try and stop him and still in a quiet voice repeat the command. Try and say it in a bright way with a lift to the tone of voice when you say 'sit'. When you want to groom his hindquarters and body you will want him standing up, so raise him to a standing position by putting your hand underneath his tummy and give him the command to stand, keeping your hand in position to prevent him sitting down again. Finally when you want him lying down to groom his chest and tummy tell him to lie down. Many puppies do not like this and it will take time and patience before he will lie quietly. Make a fuss of him but try and keep him lying on his side. Only continue for a very short time each day—he will soon learn. Never get impatient and never reward him with titbits, only praise after each part is finished.

If you can get him relaxed and at ease in his puppyhood, the business of grooming him when he has grown his full coat will be halved, and what is more you will have an obedient and happy dog. The puppies who get no training of this kind are a misery to themselves and a menace when they go to the pet shop for trimming. There are some who are so naughty that their owners cannot groom them and their coats become matted to a degree when the vet has to come and give them a sedative before they can be touched. This is all the fault of the owner not being firm at first and not the fault of the dog.

When grooming keep a watchful eye that he has not picked up any parasites—this can happen in the best regulated household. He can pick up fleas or lice from the grass and, of course, from other dogs. Should he get these pests you can either get a shampoo from your vet or the pet stores have various remedies you can brush into his coat.

Ears. It is also a good idea to get a small piece of surgical lint, wrap it round your finger, dip it in a weak solution of hydrogen peroxide and wipe it round inside his ears to keep them sweet and clean.

Teeth. These should be watched carefully especially in the toy breeds, which do not shed them as easily as the larger breeds. Give them hard biscuits such as charcoal ones to chew to help their dentation; using the

The seaside is an excellent place for any dog to enjoy himself, like these Dalmatians splashing in shallow water *(left)* but do not let your dog in the water where bathing is likely to be dangerous.

The Afghan Hound *(above)* is spectacularly beautiful but its splendid coat requires a great deal of grooming and together with the exercise a large dog built to run requires your attention for a long period each day.

When puppies feed from the same dish *(below)* the weaker and less determined may be kept back. Separate dishes would make sure they each got a fair share. These are Basset Hounds. Recent advertizing campaigns using the breed have helped to popularize them as pets. When breeds suddenly become well known in this way and desirable status symbols, it is not always to the dog's advantage. Bassets are large, low-to-the-ground sporting dogs which need a lot of exercise and many of their new owners do not appreciate this.

same kind of lint wrapped round your finger, dip it in a solution of a teaspoon of salt to one pint of water and clean all round the gums. It will help to prevent tartar forming on them. This forms very easily and if it gets bad as the dog grows older, ask your vet to remove it. It is the cause of gum deterioration and bad breath too. This applies particularly to the smaller breeds.

Eyes. A dog's eyes should not require much attention if he is in good health. Sometimes they do become a little runny, especially in puppies that are teething; in which case just wipe them dry with a piece of cotton wool moistened, but not too wet, in a weak solution of boracic lotion. Then dry them well. This can be done twice or three times a day. It is possible for any dog to get a cold in the eyes. The consequent discharge can become crusted and sore—follow the above procedure and then put a couple of drops of castor oil in them, or even wipe round the eyelids with the oil to keep them from getting dry. Gun dogs sometimes get eye injuries when hunting and the castor oil is good for these too.

In the case of a real eye injury do not go in for home treatment, go to your vet.

There is a form of night blindness, known as Progressive Retinal Atrophy, which is considered to be hereditary and only shows itself gradually. Many kennel owners have their breeding stock tested for it as there are several breeds afflicted. The dog cannot see properly and finally not at all in the dark. In some breeds it may not manifest itself until they are three to five years old but in the Irish Setter it can develop quite young. A dog tested and proved clear will not develop it later. A simple test is to take a puppy into a strange place and note whether he bumps into things as it grows dusk. The dog may also show signs of nervousness at dusk, or in the dark, which it does not display by day.

Some breeds are also being examined by their breeders for Hip Displasia which can be very painful and cause permanent lameness; it is also a hereditary disease and not apparent in a baby puppy. Both these must indicate how important it is to buy from a breeder.

Feeding. It is impossible to give exact amounts for every breed owing to their variation in size, plus the fact that, like men, each dog will vary in the amount he will require. You can only be guided by his condition. If he gets thin after you buy him, then increase the amount and vice versa. A rough quick guide is as follows:

A 10-lb dog requires $\frac{1}{2}$ lb food per day.

A 25-lb dog requires $1\frac{1}{2}$ lb food per day.

A 40-lb dog requires $1\frac{3}{4}$ lb food per day.

Bear in mind at least half of this should be *protein*, in other words, meat or fish. The rest should be carbohydrates such as biscuit meal or brown bread. As a puppy the golden rule is to give 'little and often'. At eight weeks to three months a puppy should have four meals a day at roughly four hour intervals. Two meals, generally the second and fourth, should consist of meat

Animosity between dogs and cats is often an attitude fostered primarily by their owners. The two species can in fact live very happily together *(left)*, enjoying each other's company. Playing seems to be as essential for young animals as it is for young humans. Mock attacks strengthen muscles and reflexes and in many of the actions can be seen the shadow play of the kill which, as predators, puppies would have to make for survival in the wild. In introducing a new puppy or kitten into a household where there is already an established pet, care should be taken to keep the causes of jealousy to a minimum.

Even with a large breed like the Bearded Collie *(right)* grooming is made easier if the dog is trained to sit upon a table or stool at a convenient height.

Puppies, and older dogs, like to have their toys but they will often be as happy with an old slipper or a cardboard box as with specially bought toys. This Dalmatian puppy *(below)* has settled for sacking on a string.

or fish and brown bread or biscuit meal—the latter scalded, but not made sloppy, with good stock or Marmite gravy (which is very good for him). The other two meals should be milk and cereal. At the age of three months to six months he should have three meals at roughly six hour intervals. Still keep to the two meat and biscuit meals and leave out the second milk meal. When he is aged six months to twelve months, two meals should be sufficient with a handful of hard rusks or biscuits to go to bed with.

Good red meat can be expensive but chicken is cheaper than beef these days and very nourishing for a small puppy, particularly one of the toy breeds. Incidentally these 'toys' should not be given sloppy food in the mistaken idea that their teeth are unable to cope with dry food. It can well be that much of the trouble with teeth in these small breeds is because they are given too moist foods. Their meals should be given just the same as any other breed. The biscuit should be scalded and covered over to steam, with any running gravy poured away. There are varying grades of

Kibbled meal and the wholemeal plain one is the best.

The vitamins most necessary at first are A and D which promote growth and resistance to disease. Vitamins B, C, and E are also necessary in helping to prevent skin trouble and the latter is a guard against sterility. Halibut oil capsules are good and can be given with bone meal. Of the various fish, herrings are a wonderful food as they contain so many nutriments including iodine, which is very beneficial especially to the big breeds. Just put them in a saucepan of cold water and bring them to the boil, no more. Then take them out by the tail, give them a little shake and all the flesh will come off the main backbone (the smaller side bones do not matter). Puppies usually adore them mixed with crumbled brown bread. If circumstances make it necessary for you to change the diet, do it gradually, mixing the old with the new. Strangely a change of water can sometimes cause an upset tummy in a baby puppy. If you suspect this is the reason, for a while boil the water first before giving it; boiled milk can also help with these little upsets.

Training a dog does not require special skills but it does need patience and persistence. It is always better if training is left in the hands of one member of the family. This German Shepherd Dog *(below)* has clearly learned to 'Sit'. The breed shows great aptitude for training.

Always keep your dog on a lead when out in public places but do not let it get you tied up in knots as this Bernese Mountain dog has his unhappy owner *(right)*. In fact he is a well-known dog trainer showing just what not to do for the benefit of the photographer.

INDEX

Figures in italics refer to the illustrations

Acknowledgments

The publishers would like to thank the following individuals and organizations for their kind permission to reproduce the photographs in this book:

Alpha: 59 below; Animal Photography: 4–5, 9 below, 12 above, 14, 15 above and below, 17 above and below, 19, 22 above, 25 above, 26 above and below, 31 above, 33 above, 36, 44 above, 48, 50 above and below, 52 above, 53, 55, 56 below, 57 above and below, 58, 59 above, 72, 75 above and below, 78, 79 above, 80 left, 82 above, 84 below, 85 above and below, 87, 88, 89, 91 above, 93 below, 94, 95, jacket front above right; Aspect Colour Library: 54; Colour Library International: 1, 2–3, 11 below, 29 above right, 49, 80 above, 82 below, 90; Anne Cumbers: 8, 13 below, 16 above, 20, 21 above, 22 below, 24 above, 30 below, 31 below, 33 below, 39 below, 44 below, 51, 52 below, 64, 65 above, 67 above and below, 73 below, 76, 77 above and below, 83, 93 above, jacket front below right, jacket back; Christopher Davies: 81 above; The Guide Dogs for the Blind Association: 69 above; Thomas Fall: 12 below; Keystone Press Agency: 8 top right, 84 above; Claire Leimbach: 16 below; Chris Maresch: 32, 74 left; Jim Meads: 41, 42, 43 above and below; John Moss: 10, 13 above, 30 above, 38, 40 above, 69 below, 74 above right, 81 below, 86, jacket front centre right; Dan O'Keefe: 80 below right; Pictor: 29; Picturepoint Ltd: 35; Spectrum Colour Library: 9 above, 25 below, 27, 37, 45, 66, 70, 79 below, 92, jacket front left, endpapers; Stereoscopic Photography: 68; Tony Stone Associates: 7; Syndication International: 11 above, 21 below, 91 below; Barbara Woodhouse: 23; ZEFA: 47, (M. Gnade) 61, (D. Grathwohl) 56 above, (W. L. Hamilton) 39 above, (E. Hummel) 62, (M. Nissen) 73 above, (E. Oechstein) 71, (Puck/Komeztski) 63, (Walter Schmidt) 65 below, (H. G. Trenkwalder) 24 below.